Forensic
Detection

CONTENTS

Library of Congress Cataloging-in-Publication Data

Bender, Lionel.
    Forensic detection / Lionel Bender.
      p. cm. -- (Through the microscope)
    Summary: Explores how medicine and the microscope are vital tools in aiding police investigations.
    ISBN 0-531-17250-3
    1. Medical jurisprudence--Juvenile literature. 2. Microscopy, Medical--Juvenile literature. [1. Medical jurisprudence. 2. Microscopy, Medical. 3. Microscope and microscopy.] I. Title. II. Series.
RA 1053.B39   1990
614'. 1--dc20   90-3242 CIP AC

© Aladdin Books Ltd 1990

Design David West
Children's Book Design
Author Lionel Bender
Editor Roger Vlitos
Picture Research
C. Weston-Baker
Illustrator Neil Bulpitt

*First Published in
the United States in 1990 by*
Gloucester Press,
387 Park Avenue South
New York NY 10016

Printed in Belgium

Forensic Detection

Lionel Bender

GLOUCESTER PRESS
New York: London: Toronto: Sydney

LOOKING CLOSER

Microscopes and magnifying glasses work by using lenses and light. A lens is usually a thin, circular glass, thicker in the middle, which bends rays of light so that when you look through it an object appears enlarged. A microscope uses several lenses. It will also have a set of adjustments to give you a choice over how much you want to magnify.

When we want to view something under a microscope it must be small enough to fit on a glass slide. This is put on the stage over the mirror and light is reflected through so that the lenses inside can magnify the view for us. But not all microscopes work this way. The greatest detail can be seen with an electron microscope which uses electron beams and electromagnets.

MAGNIFYING GLASS

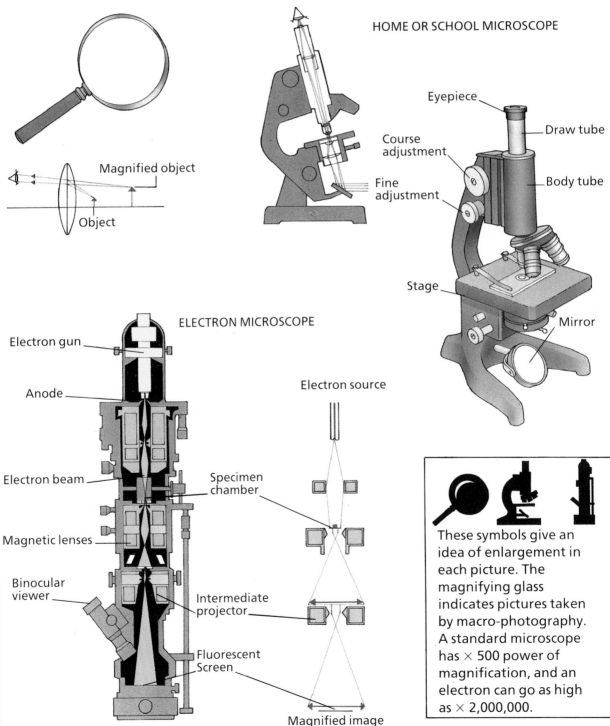

Magnified object

Object

HOME OR SCHOOL MICROSCOPE

Eyepiece

Draw tube

Course adjustment

Body tube

Fine adjustment

Stage

Mirror

ELECTRON MICROSCOPE

Electron gun

Anode

Electron beam

Magnetic lenses

Binocular viewer

Specimen chamber

Intermediate projector

Fluorescent Screen

Electron source

Magnified image

These symbols give an idea of enlargement in each picture. The magnifying glass indicates pictures taken by macro-photography. A standard microscope has × 500 power of magnification, and an electron can go as high as × 2,000,000.

INTRODUCTION

5

A microscope is used to study things too small to be seen with the naked eye. This book has pictures taken through microscopes, or with special magnifying lenses attached to cameras. Drawings appear alongside to help explain what the microscopes are showing us.

Forensic science is the study of finding, identifying, and interpreting the clues and evidence that a criminal will leave at the scene of a crime. In this book we look at the use of microscopes by forensic scientists, and show how such evidence can be used to solve a crime.

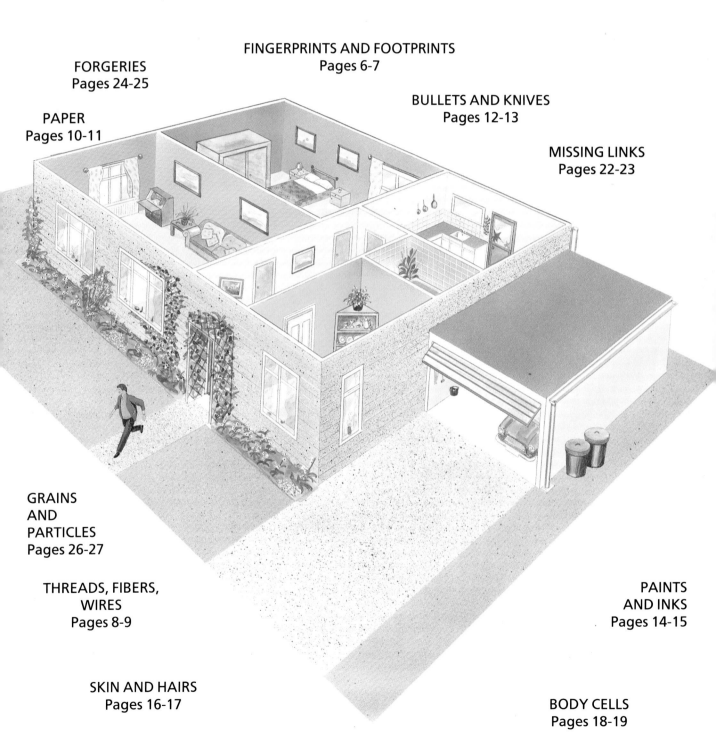

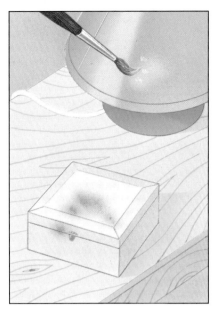

FINGERPRINTS AND FOOTPRINTS

A criminal, for example a burglar who breaks into a house to steal something, almost always leaves a trace of himself or his clothing at or around the house. It may be fingerprints on a table, or footprints in the backyard or on a carpet. It could even be tire marks made by his getaway car. Some of these clues will be visible to the naked eye, but they all need to be examined closely under a magnifying glass in order to make a positive identification. Fingerprints need to be developed and printed (see pages 28-29 for details of this procedure), and a plaster impression made of shoe or tire marks.

Shallow arch

Delta — Tight loop

Center whorl

Delta

Delta

Two loops

No two fingerprints are ever the same. This means that they can be used to identify a person. The shape of fingerprints varies greatly, as shown in the thumbprints above. Natural oils from the skin, or dirt or grease on one's fingertips, make the prints. By sprinkling fine powder on objects that a criminal may have handled, detectives can reveal an otherwise invisible fingerprint (see glass on right).

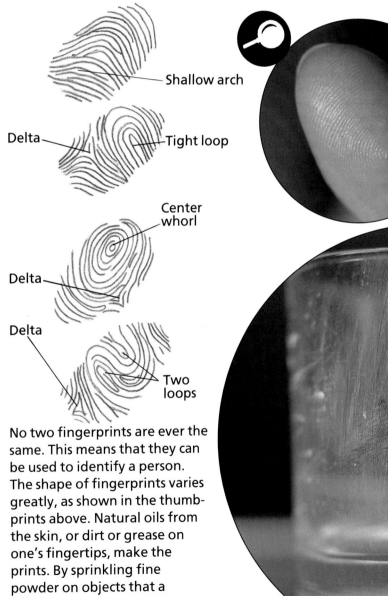

Take a look at a number of car tires and the soles of shoes of friends or relatives. You will notice that the cuts and grooves in the rubber, the tread, vary in shape, width and depth. On some tires and soles you may also see that the tread has worn away more on the inside than on the outside, or vice versa. A tire print in mud (see below and right) can reveal the make, model, and even the age or mileage of a car. The tread may also have trapped pieces of glass, grass or nails that can be matched with those found at the scene of an incident.

New tread

Old tread

Footprints, like a boot print in mud (left), and again on paper (above), reveal the type of shoes a person was wearing, how heavy, tall or short he is — and perhaps therefore his age — from which direction he came, and whether he walked or ran away. Prints that are lopsided could indicate the person was carrying something heavy, like a bag full of stolen objects. Under a magnifying glass, the maker's mark or name may be visible.

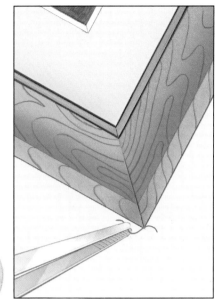

THREADS, FIBERS, WIRES

Whenever you brush up against a rough or sharp edge, such as the corner of a table, tiny threads or fibers from your clothing rub or are pulled off. Under a microscope these can often be seen to have characteristic shapes and smoothness, depending on whether they are natural fibers like cotton or silk, for example, or man-made, such as nylon, acrylic, or polyester. Each clothes manufacturer will usually keep a photographic record of the types of fibers it uses, and the police will have access to these. A forensic scientist can use these clues to match them to a suspect's clothing. Microscopic examination of cut rope fibers and wires can also reveal how, and with exactly which tool, the cuts were made.

Microscopic comparison of the ends of a length of rope can determine if the rope was severed with scissors (above) or cut by rubbing against a rough edge (below). It is even possible to detect whether the rope was cut by a right or left-handed person.

However smooth the cutting surfaces of a pair of wire-cutters appear, under a microscope they are clearly rough and jagged. Whenever a piece of wire is severed, these jagged edges leave marks called striations on the wire. Forensic scientists can compare the striations on wire-cutters found at an incident with those, say, bought from various tool manufacturers. In this way they can determine the make and model of the cutters and therefore where they were purchased. Should they find wire-cutters in a suspect's possession, microscopic examination of the striations they make in the wire will quickly reveal whether or not they were used in the crime. If the storekeeper remembers selling the cutters to the suspect, the crime is well on the way to being solved.

At a magnification of several hundred times life-size, silk threads (left) look quite different from those of pure cotton (above). The cotton threads, from a person's shirt collar, are coated with dirt and oils from the skin. Chemical studies of the oils can reveal who was wearing the shirt.

PAPER

A blackmail letter or a threatening message on notepaper may be the main clue a detective has for finding the culprit of, say, a murder, a fraud case, or a robbery. How can it be used to eliminate suspects or pick up the trail of the criminal? Firstly, it may be made from a special type of paper – recycled, wood-free or coated – or bear a unique watermark which, examined with just a magnifying glass, can reveal where it was manufactured or bought. Secondly, the notepaper may have been torn roughly into pieces so that the message could not be read again. But under a microscope the edges can be matched up, the pieces fitted together, and the message revealed. Electron microscopy can be used for closer analysis.

A criminal wrote heavily on a notepad leaving an indentation of his message on the underlying sheet of paper for anyone to find (see photo above). The torn edges of his note matched the paper remaining on the pad (right).

Handwriting experts, called graphologists, can determine whether or not a signature has been forged, or if two samples of writing have been made by the same person. Knowing this, criminals may create messages using letters or words cut from newspapers and stuck down on a sheet of paper. With the aid of microscopes and ultraviolet lighting, it is possible to look at the exact structure and source of print and paper (above). This may give a better impression of the criminal's character, or tell them where he lives, what he likes to read and so on. Identifying a watermark, like the one shown on the right, is another way that paper can be traced back to a suspect. Some types are very rare and only handled by certain suppliers.

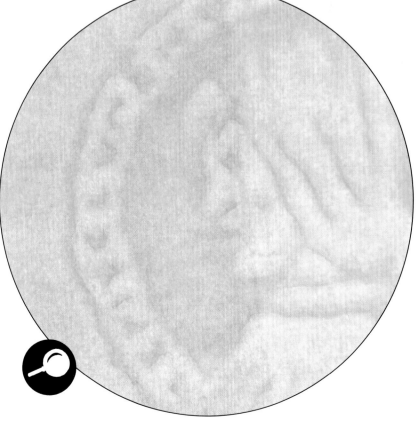

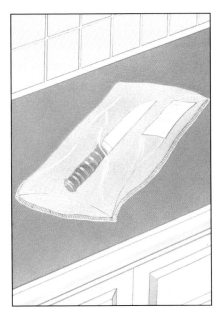

BULLETS AND KNIVES

An important part of forensic science is the study of weapons, especially firearms and the behavior of bullets or shot fired from them, which is known as ballistics. For example, scientists may be able to match the striations on a bullet found in the body of a murdered person with those on a bullet fired by a suspect's gun. By firing a revolver at sheets of cardboard from various distances and studying the different gunpowder stains and bullet hole shapes, they may be able to determine which of a group of armed criminals fired the lethal shot. A knife may be stained with blood that can be analyzed chemically. Or it may bear a unique manufacturer's mark which police can identify from a catalog or record file.

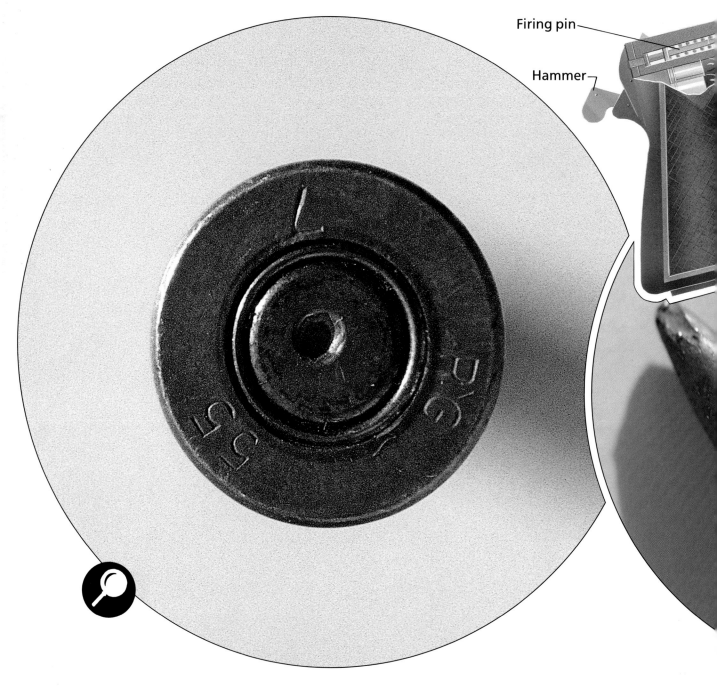

Firing pin

Hammer

When a bullet is fired, marks are left on the end of the used cartridge by the firing pin and on the sides of the bullet by the spiraled groove, or rifling, in the barrel (see diagram). A pistol taken from the scene of a crime will be fired and the used cartridges examined. Comparisons of firing pin marks (photo below left) and rifling marks (below) will be made.

Bullet cartridge and cap

Return spring

In the photo above, of two pieces of metal at a magnification of about x10, forensic scientists were able to match the scratch marks and jagged edge of a fragment of metal found in a victim's skull with the broken tip of the blade of a knife found on a suspect. Similar comparisons can be made between the ends of a used cartridge in a pistol and the bullet cap taken from a victim.

PAINTS AND INKS

When a car knocks down a pedestrian, tiny chips of paint from the vehicle may become trapped in the victim's clothing. Similarly, when a burglar breaks into a house, pieces of paint from the door or window frame may stick to his clothes. If these are found, they can link a hit-and-run driver or a burglary suspect to the scene of the crime. Perhaps the paint chips can be matched, like the pieces of a jigsaw puzzle; or the various layers of paint – primer, undercoat and topcoat – can be compared for color, thickness, and chemical composition. It is possible to identify a car model, make and year from its layers of paint. Similarly, inks and ink marks can be examined under a microscope to establish criminal connections.

The closeup photograph on the left shows a portion of someone's signature. Examination by a graphologist, someone specializing in the different kinds of handwriting, can determine what kind of pen was used and whether the writer was right or left-handed.

the su

osevelt

Here we can see a microscopic comparison of the layers of paint on a stolen car (on the left in the photo below) and on a fragment of paint found on a hit-and-run victim (on the right of the photo). Car manufacturers use the same undercoats for all models for a number of years, but the topcoats vary. The thick green topcoat on the stolen car shows that the vehicle has been resprayed. Following the accident, the car thief tried to cover up this evidence.

Loss of definition

Typewriter "E" key

Just as styles of handwriting and shapes of printed characters – letters, numbers, and symbols – are examined by forensic scientists (see page 10 and photo far left), so are ink marks. An old typewriter used to print a forged letter may leave characteristic splotches where ink from the ribbon has clogged crevices on characters such as the lower case "e" and "s." Whether the characters are smooth or rough edged, as in the sample left, may reveal whether a plastic- or a cloth-type ribbon was used.

Chipped paint work

SKIN AND HAIRS

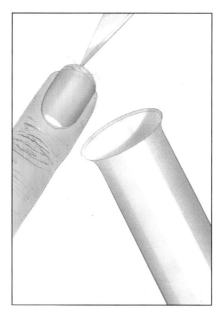

A murder victim is carefully wrapped in plastic and taken to police headquarters for examination. Care is taken to ensure that no possible clues or evidence on the body are disturbed, in this case skin cells and hairs caught under a fingernail. A pathologist, a specially trained doctor, will try to establish the cause of death. Scratches or bruises on the body, as shown in the two photographs below, indicate that the murder involved a scuffle or fight. Examination of the victim's hair may reveal unusual distortion of the individual strands, indicating poisoning by the chemical thallium. Forensic scientists will try and determine who was the murderer by microscopically examining the trapped skin cells and hairs.

This victim scratched the attacker while fighting for his, or her, life. The skin cells and hairs scratched off were later used by scientists for genetic

—Victims hands protected to preserve possible clues

fingerprinting. This involved studying the pattern made by separating the chemicals within DNA, the genetic or hereditary material in living cells which determines a person's characteristics. DNA exists in tiny chromosomes. The DNA pattern is different for everybody, with the exception of identical twins, so comparing DNA patterns from the suspect's cells and those from the victim can establish guilt.

Careful examination of scratches and bruises (photos above) can determine what kind of weapon, if any, was used. In addition, the marks made can reveal the size of an attacker's hands, and even his height and build.

Microscopic examination of human hairs, as in the photographs left and below, can provide indications of a person's age, sex, and ethnic group. It can also determine from which part of the body the hairs came.

By studying the pattern of scales from the outer surface of hair – as seen in the photo left of a human hair at a magnification of $\times 400$ – a forensic scientist can tell if it is human, or from a pet such as a cat or a dog. When hair is cut with scissors, the end is square. Hair that has been neglected tends to split at the end, as in the photo below at x125 magnification. This may link the suspect to the crime.

BODY CELLS

An obvious clue to a serious crime is a bloodstain on the victim's clothing. Microscopic studies of the blood cells can reveal if the stain also includes some blood from the attacker. The shape of blood splashes at the scene can tell how a wound was inflicted, and if the victim was moved after being stabbed or shot. In a sexual attack, traces of a man's sperm may be found on clothing. Or a severed arm or leg may be discovered, and a sample of tissue removed for further analysis. Examination of the chromosomes in the cells (see page 16), can establish at least the sex of the victim. A pathologist will study these and many other types of cells, both chemically and under a microscope, for signs of poisons, drugs, or bruising.

Normal
red blood
cells

A normal white blood cell

Blood consists of a mass of microscopic cells. Certain diseases produce abnormally shaped or roughened red and white blood cells, as in the photographs above and right. The white blood cells of women show minute drumstick-shaped projections. Such clues may link a blood sample to a suspect and thus help detectives to catch the criminal.

Sperm are a man's sex cells. An adult man produces about 200 million sperm a day. Sperm are so tiny that several hundred would easily fit onto a pinhead. The photograph, right, of human sperm, was taken at a magnification of x300. Clothing worn by a victim or suspect in an assault case is usually examined for sperm. Any found can be tested chemically to identify the man involved.

Human cells contain microscopic chromosomes. These are arranged in pairs. One special pair, the sex chromosomes, differ in males and females (see diagram below right). In females there are two large X chromosomes, and in males an X and a smaller Y chromosome. Microscopic studies of chromosomes taken from cells found at the scene of a crime, as in the photo below, can determine the sex of the person involved.

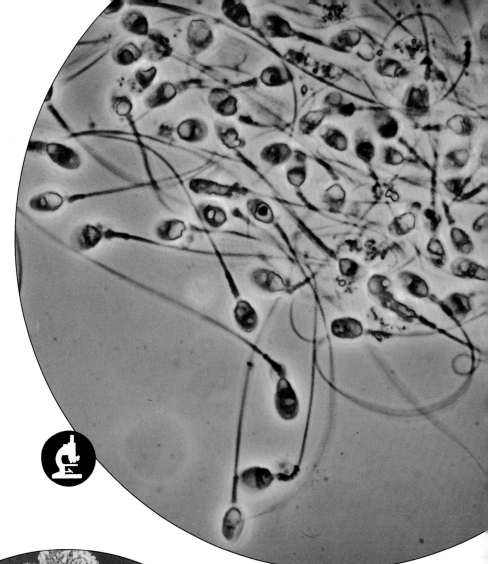

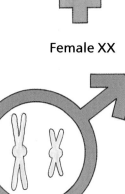

CHROMOSOMES

Female XX

Male XY

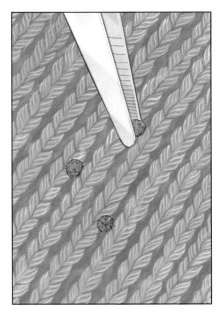

PLANT AND ANIMAL MATERIAL

An intruder who escapes through a garden or field will almost certainly pick up sticky fruits or pollen grains on his clothing from the plants that he brushes against. If he had walked on carpet in the house or in a car, hairs from a pet animal may have stuck to the soles of his shoes. Forensic scientists can use these as clues, studying them under a microscope to establish the types of plant or animal they came from. As with cloth fibers and paper, each species of flowering plant has pollen grains of a unique shape and fruits with special structures. A strand of hair can determine whether it came from a cat, dog, hamster, or rabbit.

The goosegrass or cleavers plant, with the scientific name of *Galium aparine*, has hooked fruits. These are commonly known as burrs. They each contain one seed which is dispersed by means of tiny hooks that normally stick onto an animal's fur if it brushes against the plant. Eventually, the burr splits and the seed drops out onto new ground. In the photo below at x25 magnification the burrs have become entangled in fibers of a Shetland wool pullover.

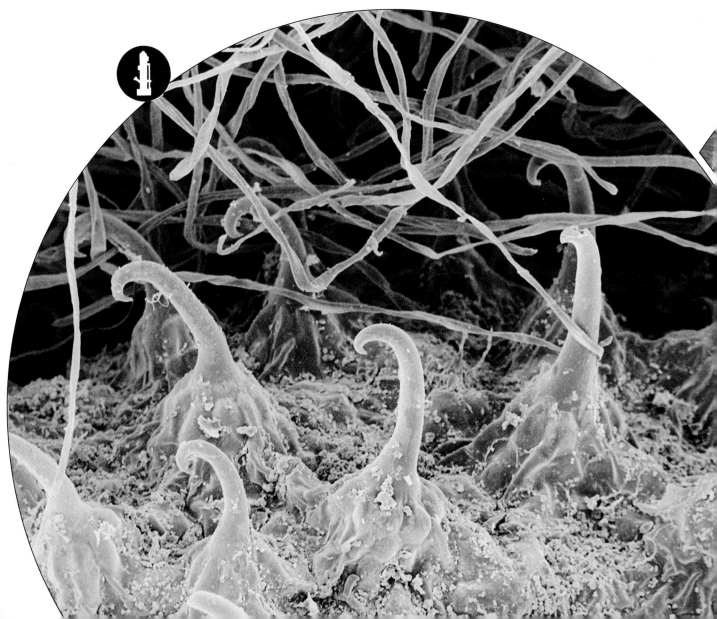

Pink
heather

Marsh
woundwort

High-powered microscopy
photographs of pollen, like
those above and above left,
reveal different shapes and
forms of the grains. Those of
the pink heather plant are
grouped in fours and the outer
wall of each grain is slightly
sculpted. Those of Marsh
woundwort have a netlike
surface pattern. Dog hairs,
shown left at a magnification of
x180, have a very distinctive
appearance.

MISSING LINKS

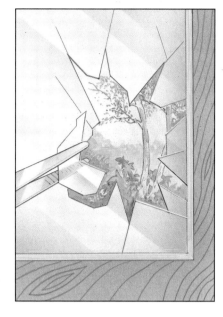

Crimes are sometimes solved with the most unlikely of clues, such as the fragments of teeth, tooth marks, pieces of torn plastic, or even fingernail clippings. Microscopic investigations can reveal, for example, whether a tooth is human, the sex and age of the person it came from, and perhaps even his or her occupation. For instance, a carpenter often holds nails and screws between his teeth and in time these leave small notches along the biting edges. Detailed examination of slivers of apple found on a suspect's clothing may reveal a match with fruit found in the kitchen where a crime occurred. On this page are three examples of such missing links and the types of crimes they may be associated with.

A gardener planting some onion bulbs in pots in a greenhouse was attacked from behind. She did not see her assailant. Detectives found fragments of onion skin trapped in the jacket of a suspect. With the help of only a magnifying glass, they were able to link them to a fragment of onion skin lying on the ground in the greenhouse. The photo below shows what they saw.

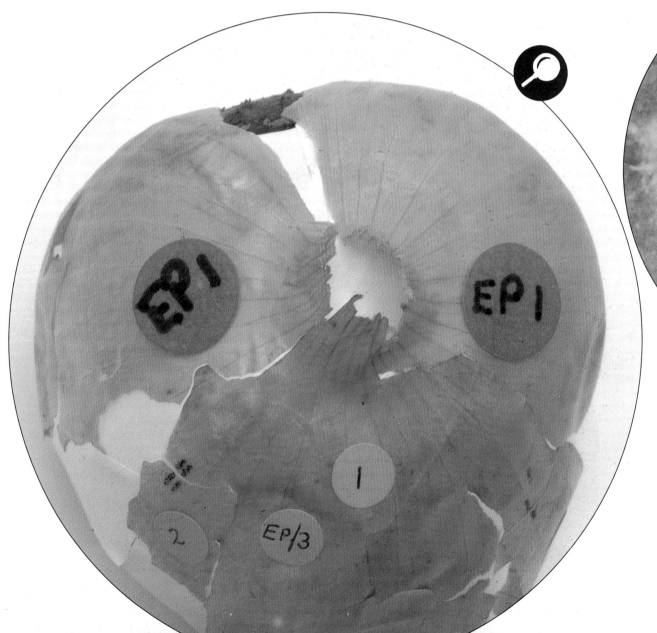

This bite mark in an apple, photo right, was the only clue forensic scientists had to go on. Examining the victim's teeth ruled her out as being the apple-eater. A plaster cast of the mark revealed an unusual set of teeth. The upper front teeth appeared to be shovel-shaped. Three of the upper back teeth had made sharp scratches on the apple skin. The teeth must have been filled and the fillings had worn to sharp edges. Investigating a dentist's records revealed the likely culprit.

Fillings

An intruder had climbed over a wire fence and stolen goods from a warehouse. No fingerprints could be found so it was likely that the criminal wore gloves. On examining the fence, detectives found some slivers of plastic (left). These must have been torn from the gloves as the intruder clambered over it. Then a suspect was found possessing a torn pair of industrial plastic gloves. Magnified study of the gloves revealed two cuts (photo far left). The slivers matched the cuts exactly (photo below).

FORGERIES

A forgery is a copy of something made to deceive or trick a person. Forgeries include copies of famous paintings and sculpture, banknotes, passports, checks, and items of jewelry. Today, paintings are usually found to be fakes by studying them with X rays – which are absorbed by the paint – or with infrared light – which penetrates the surface paint to reveal the artist's pencil or charcoal sketch. However, even the most skilled forger finds it difficult to exactly match the manufacturer's marks on jewelry or the pattern of lines on banknotes. Microscopic studies of samples of paint, identification marks, and the thickness and numbers of lines on an intricate design will reveal any telltale differences.

The most expensive gold jewelry, 22 carat, is composed of 22 parts gold and 2 parts other metals (added to give greater strength). Tests of the gold content of jewelry must be carried out by assay companies. They add their official mark, the hallmark, as in the photo above. Fake jewelry may carry the hallmark for 22 carat gold yet comprise only, say, 10 parts gold to 14 parts other metals. A suspicious-looking hallmark will prompt a forensic scientist to test the jewelry and so reveal the truth about the metal.

Paintings are usually forged for financial reasons. A copy of a masterpiece may deceive an art dealer, who will pay millions of dollars in order to have the painting in his private gallery. But there are cases of forgeries made just to make a fool of art critics, who largely determine the popularity of a painter and thus the market price of their work. Sometimes the forgers have left glaring clues so that their trick will be discovered later on. The most famous of oil painters have a unique painting style and technique, just as handwriting differs from person to person. Close examination of their work can reveal the brushstrokes, as in the photo above. As paintings age, the layers of paint and the protective varnish layer tend to crack. The extent and pattern of the cracking, as in the photo left, can determine if a painting is an old original or a modern fake copy.

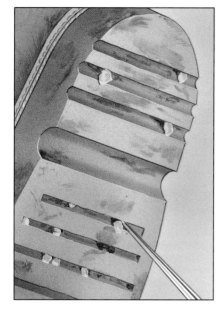

GRAINS AND PARTICLES

Just as scientists can identify threads and fibers under a microscope, they can also distinguish between tiny objects. The scanning electron microscopic pictures shown here reveal the smoothness and regularity of the shapes of some grains and the unevenness of others. Grains and particles such as these may be found trapped in a suspect's clothing or in the grooves on the soles of shoes. Matching these to grains found at the scene of a crime or in a stolen car, for instance, may help to identify the guilty person or determine where and how a crime was committed. Examination of crystals can reveal whether grit found in the bottom of a teacup is undissolved sugar or ground glass used to try and harm a person.

At a magnification of more than x40, these salt grains (below and left) look quite different on account of their different means of production. Those on the left are rough grains formed as drops of sea (salty) water were dried in the sun. Those below are grains of table salt made smooth by boiling so that they will pour easily from a salt shaker. Sea salt may be picked up by a person's shoes on a beach and table salt from a kitchen floor.

To hide evidence such as dust brushed off furniture or particles picked up by his shoes and then left on his car seat or floor mat, a burglar may have vacuumed his car. Forensic scientists examining the contents of the cleaner-bag will take away any particles they find for microscopic examination. In this case they were able to match sand and grit particles (left and far left) from the bag with those from a path to the burgled house.

PRACTICAL PROJECTS

You can discover a great deal about how forensic scientists work with just a magnifying glass. But to see greater detail you will need a home microscope (see page 4). The objects you wish to study must be mounted on a glass slide. They must be thin enough to allow light to shine through them. You may need to cut very thin slices of material or to tease them out until they are very fine. To pick out different types of structures, you will need to stain your specimens. The way to do this is outlined below. If you are going to try something which is a bit tricky, it is worth getting help from an adult. You may be able to start your studies with some ready-made slides bought from a microscope supplier.

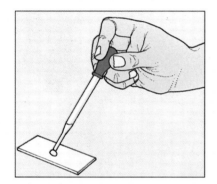

To prepare a cell slide, place a drop of clean water containing the cells on the glass.

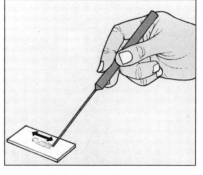

With a wire loop that has been sterilized in a flame, spread the fluid thinly and let it dry.

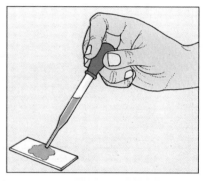

Add a small drop of staining dye to the cells and leave for a few minutes.

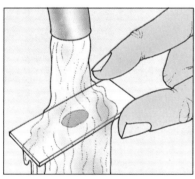

Wash off the dye with water or alcohol. You can stain with another, contrasting dye.

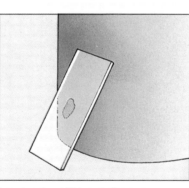

Leave the slide to dry. You can speed up drying by gently warming the slide over a flame.

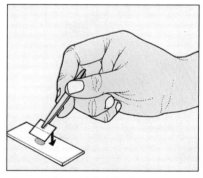

Place a cover slip (a thin square of glass) over the stained cells, using a pair of tweezers.

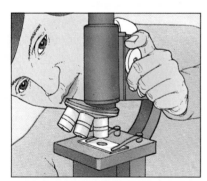

Put the slide on the microscope stage and position the mirror to give you good illumination.

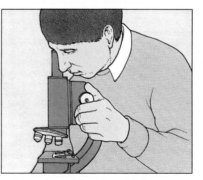

Select the objective lens you want, then move the eyepiece up and down to focus. Start at the lowest magnification.

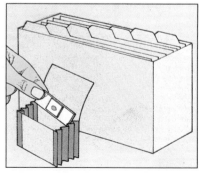

Keep your prepared slides in a wallet made from a folded sheet of cardboard, which will protect them from dust.

Arrange some specimens of sugar, pollen, and tea so that you can see whether your friends can identify them with just a magnifying glass.

With a magnifying glass, compare the edges of sheets of paper, as above, cut with scissors, the edge of a ruler or torn with your hands. See if you can fit together small pieces of paper torn from a single sheet.

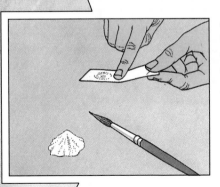

Ask some of your friends or relatives to make fingerprints on a glass tabletop. Brush talcum powder very gently into and around the prints. Blow away any surplus powder. Then press a piece of sticky tape onto each print. Finally, peel the tape off carefully and their fingerprints will come up with it. Stick the tape onto black cardboard or paper to examine it better. Compare the prints with fingertips and see if you can match prints to people.

MICROPHOTOGRAPHY

Forensic scientists collect clues and evidence at the scene of a crime and take them back to the laboratory for further examination. They usually arrive at the scene of a crime with a box full of plastic collecting bottles, tubes and envelopes; tags for listing objects; a camera to photograph the position of items such as a dead body, bloodstains or weapons; a fingerprint kit; and scissors, tweezers etc. Back at the laboratory they photograph microscope slide images to check them against police records and for use as evidence in court. This is a long and hard job. However, the telltale evidence uncovered by such painstaking police procedures has helped put many a criminal behind bars.

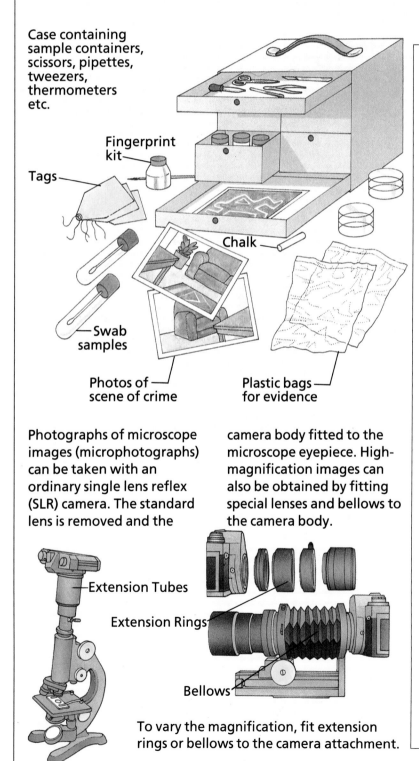

Case containing sample containers, scissors, pipettes, tweezers, thermometers etc.

Fingerprint kit

Tags

Chalk

Swab samples

Photos of scene of crime

Plastic bags for evidence

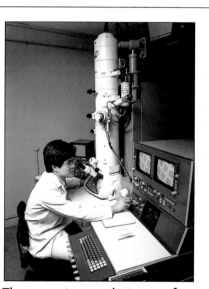

There are two main types of electron microscope. In a transmission type (TEM), a beam of electrons is passed through a very thin slice of tissue and an image is produced on a screen. In a scanning electron microscope (SEM), a fine beam of electrons is moved across the surface of the tissue for reflections to be collected and used to create an image on a television type of screen. Using an SEM, realistic 3-D images are produced. But as with all types of microscope specimens, the tissues and organs are no longer alive. The slide preparation process kills live cells. The colors on photos produced using an SEM are false colors added in processing.

Photographs of microscope images (microphotographs) can be taken with an ordinary single lens reflex (SLR) camera. The standard lens is removed and the camera body fitted to the microscope eyepiece. High-magnification images can also be obtained by fitting special lenses and bellows to the camera body.

Extension Tubes

Extension Rings

Bellows

To vary the magnification, fit extension rings or bellows to the camera attachment.

GLOSSARY

ballistics The study of the movement of objects, such as bullets, under the force of gravity.

blood A red fluid that travels around the body in the veins and arteries. Blood is made up of two types of blood cells, the red and white corpuscles, and a straw colored liquid, the plasma. Blood is pumped around the body by the heart and gushes forth from a cut. The shape and size of bloodstains can tell forensic scientists something about how a cut or injury was sustained.

cell The smallest unit or building block of living things. Most cells in the human body are about 0.001 inches across and can be seen only with a microscope. They differ greatly in shape and form and can reveal which part of the body a sample of flesh comes from.

chromosome Part of the cell nucleus which determines a person's appearance.

crystal A regularly shaped structure created by the precise way in which some atoms combine together in chemical elements and compounds. Diamond is a crystal formed by the regular bonds between atoms of carbon. Salt grains get their cube shape from the regular links between sodium and chlorine atoms. Various chemical compounds have unique and characteristic crystal shapes.

DNA Short for deoxyribonucleic acid. DNA is a chemical blueprint for living things. It carries coded information that determines the features of a creature and ensures that these are copied and passed on to any offspring.

fingerprint The mark left by the tiny ridges of a person's fingers and thumbs on an object they touch or pick up. The mark is made by natural oils from the skin, or by grease or ink covering the fingertips.

forensic Term relating to the use of clues and evidence in a court of law. Forensic medicine is the use of medical knowledge in legal problems.

graphology The study of determining a person's character from their handwriting.

hallmark An official mark used to denote the purity of expensive jewelry made from the metals gold, silver, and platinum.

magnification The number of times the diameter, or distance across, something appears to be enlarged or made bigger.

pathologist A doctor specializing in determining the cause of death, illness or disease.

striations Fine lines along the surface of an object. However smooth a surface may appear to the naked eye, under a microscope many bumps, grooves and striations can usually be seen.

watermark A special pattern, picture or mark made in the fibers of a sheet or paper by the manufacturer as a sign of quality.

WEIGHTS AND MEASURES

mm = millimeters 10mm = 0.4 inch
cm = centimeter 100cm = 1m = 3.3 feet
m = meter 1000m = 1km = 0.6 mile
km = kilometer
lb = pound

g = gram 1000g = 1kg = 2lb 3oz
kg = kilogram
0.1 = 1/10
0.01 = 1/100
0.001 = 1/1000

INDEX

Photographic Credits:
Cover and pages 6 all, 7 all, 8 left and bottom, 10 bottom 12, 13 bottom, 14 both, 16 both, 23 top, 24, 25 all and 29 top and bottom: Roger Vlitos; title page and pages 8 right, 9 top, 11 top, 17 both, 18 both, 19 both, 20, 21 all, 26 and 27 all: Science Photo Library; 9 bottom, 10 top, 13 top, 15, 22, 23 middle left and middle right and bottom: Forensic Science Laboratories, Metropolitan Police; 29 middle: Paul Brierley.

PRINTED IN BELGIUM BY proost INTERNATIONAL BOOK PRODUCTION